# DON QUIXOTE

Pablo Ley's plays include *Se està haciendo muy tarde* (Sant Martí de Teatre prize, Mercat de les Flors, 1988) and *Paisaje sin casas* (Marqués de Bradomín 1990 prize). His adaptations include *Faust version 3.0* (from Goethe's original with La Fura dels Baus), *The Threepennyopera* (Teatre Grec, Barcelona), *Barbaric Comedies* (La Nave de Sagunto, Valencia), *Homage to Catalonia* (West Yorkshire Playhouse, Leeds; Northern Stage, Newcastle; MC93 Bobigny, Paris; and Teatre Romea, Barcelona), *Festen* (Teatre Romea) and most recently *2666* (Teatre Lliure). He collaborates regularly with Spain's leading theatre directors Calixto Bieito, Bigas Lunas and Joesp Galindo.

Colin Teevan's plays include *Peer Gynt* (Dundee Rep/National Theatre of Scotland), *How Many Miles to Basra?* (West Yorkshire Playhouse), *The Bee*, co-written with Hideki Noda (Soho Theatre), *Missing Persons* (Assembly Rooms/Trafalgar Studios), *Alcmaeon in Corinth* (Live! Theatre Newcastle), *Monkey!* (Young Vic), *The Walls* (National Theatre), *Švejk* (Gate/The Duke, Broadway), *Vinegar and Brown Paper* (Abbey Theatre) and *The Big Sea* (Riverside Studios). His translations include Giuseppe Manfridi's *Cuckoos* (Gate/Barbican), Edoardo Erba's *Marathon* (Gate), *Iph…*, a version of *Iphigenia in Aulis* and *Bacchai* (National Theatre). All are published by Oberon Books.

Miguel de Cervantes
# DON QUIXOTE

Adapted for the stage by
Colin Teevan & Pablo Ley

OBERON BOOKS
LONDON

WWW.OBERONBOOKS.COM

First published in this adaptation in 2007 by Oberon Books Ltd
521 Caledonian Road, London N7 9RH
Tel: +44 (0) 20 7607 3637 / Fax: +44 (0) 20 7607 3629
e-mail: info@oberonbooks.com
www.oberonbooks.com

A catalogue record for this book is available from the British
Library.

Cover design by West Yorkshire Playhouse

PB ISBN: 9781840028027
E ISBN: 9781786822086

eBook conversion by Lapiz Digital Services, India.

Visit www.oberonbooks.com to read more about all our books and
to buy them. You will also find features, author interviews and news
of any author events, and you can sign up for e-newsletters so that
you're always first to hear about our new releases.

# Characters

*in order of appearance*

CIDE HAMETE BENENGELI
NIECE
HOUSEKEEPER
PRIEST
BARBER NICOLAS
DON QUIXOTE
SANCHO PANZA
TERESA PANZA
SANCHICO PANZA
SANCHICA PANZA
BASQUE MONK
AMBROSIO
MARCELA
INNKEEPER'S DAUGHTER
MARITORNES
INNKEEPER
THE CAPTIVE
MULE-DRIVER
INNKEEPER'S WIFE
OFFICER
GUARD
GINES DE PASAMONTE
THE DEVIL
CARDENIO

FERNANDO
LUSCINDA
PRIEST
DOROTEA
FIRST DULCINEA
SECOND DULCINEA
MONTESINOS
THE DUCHESS
THE DUKE
THE ECCLESIASTIC
DEMON
MERLIN
THIRD DULCINEA
FOURTH DULCINEA
ALTISADORA
COUNTESS TRIFALDI
MASTER PEDRO
THE FALSE QUIXOTE
DON ANTONIO
HEAD
A WOMAN
NEXT WOMAN
GENTLEMAN

*and*

SHEPHERDS, A PHANTASMAGORICAL VOICE, DEATH, AN ANGEL,
AN EMPEROR, A QUEEN, A KNIGHT, MAIDENS IN MOURNING,
LADY BELERMA, BEARDED HANDMAIDS, and A NOTARY.

This adaptation of *Don Quixote* was first performed on 22 September 2007 at the Quarry Theatre, West Yorkshire Playhouse, with the following company:

SANCHO PANZA,  Tony Bell

SANCHICO,  Alasdair Craig

BARBER,  Stephen Casey

CIDE,  Andrew Dennis

TERESA,  Rachel Donovan

DON QUIXOTE,  Greg Hicks

PRIEST,  Alan McMahon

NIECE,  Caitlin Mottram

SANCHICA,  Laura Power

HOUSEKEEPER,  Phoebe Soteriades

All other parts were played by members of the company.

*Director* Josep Galindo

*Designer* Gideon Davey

*Video Designer* Mic Pool

*Lighting Designer* Charles Balfour

*Composer* David Benke

*Sound Designer* Mike Beer

*Fight Director* Kate Waters

*Casting Director* Kay Magson

*Assistant Director* Kathryn Ind

# Act One

## PROLOGUE

NIECE: The reason for the unreason to which my reason is subjected so weakens my reason that it's with reason I complain of your beauty.

CIDE HAMETE BENENGELI: In a village in La Mancha, the name of which I don't recall, there lived a gentleman named Quixada or Quexada. He was one of those gentlemen who has a lance and a shield on the wall and a skinny nag in the stable. He was about fifty years old, his complexion was leathery and his bones were lean. He was an early riser and liked to hunt, but mostly he spent his time reading books of chivalry. So lost was he in his reading, from dusk to dawn, from sunrise to sunset, that his brains dried up like old beans in the sun, and he lost his mind. So that it seemed both reasonable and necessary, both for the sake of his honour and service to his state, to become a knight-errant. And so, early one July morning, having buckled on the rusty armour of his great-grandfather and decided to be enamoured of a lady, some peasant girl called Aldonza Lorenzos, whom he now called Dulcinea del Toboso, our knight, Don Quixote de La Mancha, left his home, mounted his charger Rocinante, and set off across the Manchegan plains in search of adventure.

## THE LIBRARY

HOUSEKEEPER: Three days and not a sign of him, nor his old horse, nor his armour. Lord help us! As true as the death I owe God, those damned books of chivalry he's always at have completely turned his mind.

NIECE: Do you know, father, my uncle used to spend two days and nights non-stop, reading and re-reading those god-awful books of misadventures? And when he'd done he'd throw the book away, grab his sword and start thrusting and slashing at the walls. Then, when he was tired, he'd say he'd killed four giants and the sweat that poured from him was the blood from the wounds he'd received. Then he'd drink a jug of cold water and come over calm, saying the water was a precious potion which the wise Flanflan, or somesuch, a magician friend of his, had brought him. You should burn those books like heretics.

PRIEST: Hear, hear! And with God's help we shall not let one more day pass without trying them and sentencing them to the flames.

HOUSEKEEPER: Take this, your reverence, some hyssop and some holy water, and baptise the room so that none of the enchanters in these books can put a spell on us.

PRIEST: Master Nicolas, hand them to me one by one so we can consider their contents.

NIECE: Why should we pardon any? Throw them all out the window. Make a bonfire in the courtyard.

PRIEST: *Amadis of Gaul.* The first book of chivalry printed in Spain. It should be condemned as the founder of the vile sect.

BARBER NICOLAS: But I've heard it's the best of the lot, so perhaps it should be pardoned.

PRIEST: Well said, Master Nicolas, let it be spared.

NIECE: But...?

PRIEST: For the present. What's that one, next to it?

BARBER NICOLAS: The *Exploits of Esplandian,* the legitimate son of Amadis of Gaul. Are they all about Amadis and his family?

PRIEST: Out the window with the whole tribe of them.

BARBER NICOLAS: Yes.

NIECE: Yes! Yes!

HOUSEKEEPER: Give them here, then.

PRIEST: Who's this mighty fellow?

BARBER NICOLAS: Don Olivante de Laura.

PRIEST: A silly and arrogant work. Into the courtyard with it!

BARBER NICOLAS: *Part One of the Great History of the Spirited and Sporting Prince Felixmarte of Hyrcania and his Extraordinary Birth.*

PRIEST: To the yard, I say, for the stiffness and dryness of his style.

HOUSEKEEPER: My pleasure, you reverence.

BARBER NICOLAS: *The Knight Platir.*

PRIEST: An old book, but age is no reason for clemency.

BARBER NICOLAS: *The Knight of the Cross.*

NIECE: Out!

BARBER NICOLAS: *The Mirror of Chivalry.*

NIECE: Out! Out! Out!

BARBER NICOLAS: *Ludovico Ariosto.*

PRIEST: I will not read Ariosto in any language but the original.

BARBER NICOLAS: Well this must be in Italian because it's all Greek to me.

PRIEST: Show me? Bellisima!

NIECE: Burn them! Burn them all!

PRIEST: God help me! *Tirante el Blanco!* Not Tirante! This is the best book in the world. In this one knights eat and sleep, and die in their beds, and make their wills before dying. Sensible knights, reasonable knights, good knights.

NIECE: Good night to them all!

PRIEST: Take it home with you, Master Nicolas, and read it, and you will see what I say is true. What's that one?

CIDE HAMETE BENENGELI: *La Galatea*, by Miguel de Cervantes.

PRIEST: Cervantes?

CIDE HAMETE BENENGELI: He was a friend of mine years ago, though I know he's more versed in misfortune than in fiction. His book has a certain imagination. Perhaps in the future it will achieve the mercy it is denied now.

PRIEST: Set it aside.

BARBER NICOLAS: I'll do that, your reverence.

PRIEST: Now wall up the book room so when your master comes to, he won't be able to find them.

*Enter DON QUIXOTE, he cannot find his library.*

HOUSEKEEPER: What is it you're looking for, your worship?

DON QUIXOTE: My library, good housekeeper, my books.

HOUSEKEEPER: What library? The Devil himself came and took it away.

NIECE: No, uncle, it wasn't the Devil but a magician who came the night after the day you went out on the road in search of adventures. And when he arrived, he dismounted the serpent he rode and entered the room. What he did in there we don't know, but after a while he left, filling the house with smoke. And when we went to see what he'd done we saw neither books nor room, but as he was leaving, he said in clear voice that because of a personal grudge he held against the owner of the books, he'd done mischief in that house that would be discovered by-and-by.

HOUSEKEEPER: He said his name was the Great Tortilla.

DON QUIXOTE: You are mocking me, housekeeper.

HOUSEKEEPER: I'm sorry, your worship.

DON QUIXOTE: He must have said Gazpacho. The Great Gazpacho.

HOUSEKEEPER: That was it. Because he said that this was only for starters.

DON QUIXOTE: Gazpacho is a powerful magician, and a great enemy of mine. He knows that at some point in the future I shall engage in single combat with a knight he favours, and that I'll defeat him, and that he'll be unable to prevent it. That's why he's done this. Any opportunity he has.

NIECE: We don't doubt it, uncle, so, wouldn't it be wiser to stay at home instead of roaming the wide world looking for trouble?

DON QUIXOTE: My dear niece, how little you understand! I shall pluck the beard of any man or wizard who so much as dreams he can touch a hair upon my head.

## THE SQUIRE

*Enter SANCHO with TERESA, SANCHICO and SANCHICA.*

HOUSEKEEPER: Get out, you yard dog, we don't need anyone leading our master astray again.

SANCHO PANZA: You old hag of a housekeeper! The only one doing any leading astray round here is your master. He's the one who promised me an island.

NIECE: An island! I hope your island sticks in your fat throat and chokes you.

HOUSEKEEPER: That's as may be, but you still can't come in. Go govern your own home and stop trying to govern islands, you bladder of badness, you sack of sin.

DON QUIXOTE: It saddens me, Sancho, that you insist that it's I who lures you away. Together shall we venture out, together shall we journey, together shall we share a single fortune and a single fate.

SANCHO PANZA: But a knight-errant should suffer the misfortunes, not his squire.

DON QUIXOTE: But what of *'quando caput dolet'*, Sancho?

SANCHO PANZA: Quando quappit what?

DON QUIXOTE: It means that when the head aches, the body hurts too. Since I am your lord and master, I am your head, so any misfortune that touches me will cause you pain, and vice versa.

SANCHO PANZA: (*Mimicking.*) 'You must know, Sancho my friend, quando crappit donut...'

TERESA PANZA: Ever since you became a knight's squire, Sancho, your talk is so fancy no one can understand you.

SANCHO PANZA: It's enough that God understands me, wife. Besides, we're not going to a wedding, but to travel the wide world to battle with monsters, dragons and giants.

TERESA PANZA: And I believe, husband, that squires errant don't earn their bread for nothing. May the Lord deliver you from evil.

SANCHO PANZA: I swear if I'm not made governor of an island soon, let me drop down dead right here.

TERESA PANZA: The Devil take all governorships. The best sauce in the world is hunger, and since the poor have plenty of that, they always eat it with great pleasure. And what about your children? Sanchico's already fifteen and ought to start school. And Sanchica keeps dropping hints she wants a husband.

SANCHO PANZA: When God grants me an island to govern I'll marry Sanchica so high up the Queen herself shall have to call her 'ma'am'.

TERESA PANZA: You'll not, she'll marry an equal. You can't raise her from wooden clogs to cork-soled shoes. Poor girl won't know who she is.

SANCHO PANZA: She just needs to practise for a year or two and she'll be a perfect lady.

TERESA PANZA: Over my dead body will my daughter be a lady! You take care of the money and leave the marrying to me!

SANCHO PANZA: Come here to me, you wife of Barrabas, do you not want our grandchildren to be called 'lord' and 'lady'?

TERESA PANZA: Listen to yourself! Do what you want, go have your adventures with your Don Quixote, make her a duchess or a princess but don't count on my support.

*Exit TERESA.*

SANCHO PANZA: Sir! Don Quixote, sir!

DON QUIXOTE: What is it, Sancho?

SANCHO PANZA: Sir, can you give me something to placate my wife?

DON QUIXOTE: Reward shall come in time, and, if it doesn't, I have promised you some wages.

SANCHO PANZA: But what exactly were a knight's squire's wages?

## THE ROAD

DON QUIXOTE: Everyone halt and confess that there is no woman in the world more beautiful than the Empress of La Mancha, the peerless Dulcinea del Toboso.

CIDE HAMETE BENENGELI: But sir, we don't know this lady. Show her to us and if she's as beautiful as you say, we'll gladly confess the truth of it.

DON QUIXOTE: If I were to show her to you, what would be the point in having to swear to such an obvious truth? You must believe, confess and swear to the truth without seeing her. That's the point.

CIDE HAMETE BENENGELI: But I beg you, at least show us a portrait, even a miniature, just so we know that she's not humpbacked and blind in one eye and brimstone doesn't ooze from the other.

DON QUIXOTE: Nothing oozes from her, nor is she humpbacked. She's as upright as a peak of the Guadarrama. You'll pay for your blasphemy.

*DON QUIXOTE goes to attack his interlocutors but he trips and they are gone.*

Flee not cowards, wretches, come back! It's not my fault I fell, but my horse's, come back... Look Sancho, fortune is guiding our affairs better than we could have hoped. Look there, thirty or even more monstrous giants, all of whom I intend to engage with in battle and kill and with their treasure as our spoils, we'll begin to make our fortunes. This is a just war, for it is God's wish that this evil race be wiped off the face of the earth.

SANCHO PANZA: But what giants, your worship?

DON QUIXOTE: Those ones there, with the long arms.

SANCHO PANZA: I don't see giants, your worship, but windmills. Those aren't arms but sails.

DON QUIXOTE: You're obviously not used to the business of adventures. Those are giants, and if you're afraid, take yourself off and pray, while I engage them in fierce and unequal combat.

*DON QUIXOTE addresses the windmills.*

Do not flee you cowards, it is but a single knight who attacks you!

*A gust of wind turns the sails.*

Even if you wave your arms more than the hundred-armed Briareus, I'll bring you to your knees.

*He charges the windmills but is defeated by the turning sails.*

SANCHO PANZA: Did I not tell your worship they were windmills?

DON QUIXOTE: Matters of war are subject to continual change, Sancho. The same Gazpacho who stole my library has transformed the giants into windmills to deprive me of the glory of slaying them.

SANCHO PANZA: And I suppose I must believe everything your worship says, even though you're lopsided after your fall.

DON QUIXOTE: I am, but I refuse to complain, for it's not usual for knights-errant to complain. Even if their guts are spilling out all over the floor.

SANCHO PANZA: I hope the same does not apply to knights' squires, I usually complain about the smallest thing.

DON QUIXOTE: Sancho, either I'm deceived, or this will be our most famous adventure. Look! Now they are undoubtedly enchanters who have captured a princess, and I must do everything in my power to right this wrong.

SANCHO PANZA: Are you sure, your worship? It might be the Devil who's deceiving you.

DON QUIXOTE: Wicked unnatural creatures, release this instant the noble princess you hold captive or prepare to receive a swift death as punishment.

BASQUE MONK: Listen, knight pal, watch who you're calling wicked! We're just poor mendicant monks.

DON QUIXOTE: Do not try and talk your way out of it, I know what you are, you filthy rabble.

BASQUE MONK: I'm telling you, pal, if you don't get out of our road, I kill you dead.

DON QUIXOTE: If you were a gentleman, as you obviously are not, I would already have punished your audacity, base creature.

BASQUE MONK: Me, no gentleman? I'm Basque, pal, and proud. And we Basques are a noble people, and if you don't agree, I'll burst your head.

*DON QUIXOTE prepares for battle.*

DON QUIXOTE: O lady of my soul, Dulcinea del Toboso, flower of beauty, come to the aid of this thy knight.

*They attack each other.*

CIDE HAMETE BENENGELI: Finally Don Quixote had met someone who could experience the valour of his mighty arm. Some authors claim that this adventure was apocryphal, but, according to what I have been able to discover in the annals of La Mancha, this was his first great fight. And with such fury did Don Quixote bring his sword down upon his opponent's head, blood began to spout from the Basque's nose, mouth, ears. His body fell to the ground.

*Darkness.*

SANCHO PANZA: O flower of chivalry, a single lethal blow has laid you low in your prime! O glory of La Mancha, which, with you absent, will be overrun by evildoers. O humble with the proud and proud with the humble, attacker of dangers, endurer of insults, enamoured without cause. O knight-errant, the best that can be said of any man.

*DON QUIXOTE lies as if dead.*

DON QUIXOTE: Perhaps, Sancho my friend, it would be wise to allow this current unfortunate configuration of the stars to pass. This is how the evil magician, my enemy, makes things disappear and seem what they are not.

## THE MOUNTAINS

*A procession of shepherds carrying a body. Enter MARCELA.*

AMBROSIO: Are you come, by chance, cruel basilisk of these mountains, to see if in your presence blood will flow from the wounds of this wretched being your cruelty has robbed of life? Or is it to exult over the cruel work of your humours?

MARCELA: I come not, Ambrosio, for the purpose you have named, but to defend myself and to prove how unreasonable are all those who blame me for Chrysostom's death. Heaven has made me, so you say, beautiful, and so much so that in spite of yourselves my beauty leads you to love me; and for the love you show me you say that I am bound to love you. Now I know that everything beautiful attracts love, but I cannot see how, by reason of being loved, that which is loved for its beauty is bound to love that by which it is loved, since it may easily happen that the lover of that which is beautiful may be itself ugly, and ugliness being unlovable, it is very absurd to say, 'I love you because you are beautiful, you must love me even though I'm ugly.' But supposing the beauty equal on both sides, it still does not follow that the inclinations must also be alike, for it is not every beauty that excites love, some but pleasing the eye without winning the affection. And if every sort of beauty excited love, the will would wander vaguely to and fro, like a leaf in the wind, unable to make any clear choice.

*Exit MARCELA.*

DON QUIXOTE: Let no one, whatever his rank, dare follow the beautiful Marcela, or they shall incur my fiercest indignation.

## THE ROAD

*Night. Long pause.*

SANCHO PANZA: I know, to make the journey shorter and the darkness less dark, I'll you a story which, if I can manage to get through it and nobody interferes with the telling, is the best of stories. Listen, your worship, I'm going to begin. Right. Ahem. So. In a certain village in Estremadura, the name of which I can't recall, there lived a goatherd, that is to say, one who tended goats. This goatherd, according to the story, was called Lope Ruiz, and this Lope Ruiz was in love with a shepherdess called Torralva, and this shepherdess called Torralva was the daughter of a rich grazier, and this rich grazier –

DON QUIXOTE: If you tell your story by repeating everything twice, Sancho, it will take two days to finish. Get on with it!

SANCHO PANZA: That's our customary way of telling stories. I can't tell it in any other way, and it's not right for your worship to ask me to change my customs.

DON QUIXOTE: Tell it as you will then, since I have no choice but to listen to you.

SANCHO PANZA: As I was saying, this goatherd was in love with Torralva the shepherdess, who was a wild buxom lass with something of the look of a man about her. She had a little moustache; I can see her now.

DON QUIXOTE: You knew her?

SANCHO PANZA: I did not, but the man who told me the story said it was so true and certain that when I told it to another I could swear blind I had seen it myself. And so, in the course of time, the Devil, who never sleeps and throws everything into confusion, contrived that the love the goatherd bore the shepherdess turned to hate. The reason was some little jealousy she'd caused him. But from that time forward, so much did the goatherd hate her that in order to be rid of her, he determined to leave the region altogether and go where he'd never have to clap eyes on her again. Meanwhile, Torralva, the shepherdess, when she found out, was immediately smitten with love for him.

DON QUIXOTE: That's generally the way with women, to scorn the one that loves them, and love the one that hates them.

SANCHO PANZA: And so the goatherd and his goats crossed the plains of Estremadura to get to the Kingdom of Portugal. Torralva went after him, barefoot and at a distance. The goatherd came with his goats to cross over the river Guadiana, but at the spot there was neither ferry nor boat, nor anyone to carry him or his goats to the other side. This really angered him since he knew that Torralva was approaching and her tears and pleadings would get on his wick. Luckily, therefore, he found a fisherman who had a boat. Unluckily, however, it was so small that it could only hold one man and one goat. All the same, the fisherman agreed to carry Lope Ruiz, the goatherd, and his three hundred goats across. The fisherman got into the boat and carried one goat over. He came back and carried another over – let your worship keep count of the goats the fisherman takes across, if one escapes that'll be an end of the story, and I won't be able to tell another word of it. Oh and yes, the landing place on the other side was muddy and slippery, and the fisherman lost a great deal of time in going and coming; still he returned for another goat, and another goat, and another goat –

DON QUIXOTE: Let's take it for granted that he brought them all across. If you keep going and coming like this it will take you a year to finish.

SANCHO PANZA: How many have crossed so far?

DON QUIXOTE: How the devil do I know?

SANCHO PANZA: But I told you to keep a good count. That's an end of the story, then. I can't go on.

DON QUIXOTE: Why? Is it so important to the story to know exactly how many goats have crossed over that if there's one mistake, you can't go on?

SANCHO PANZA: No, but when I asked your worship to tell me how many goats had crossed, and you answered you didn't know, at that moment the whole story went clean out of my head. Pity, it was a good story.

*Pause.*

DON QUIXOTE: So, that's the end of it?

SANCHO PANZA: It's as dead as my mother.

*Pause.*

DON QUIXOTE: In truth, that's one of the most original stories I've ever come across.

## THE INN

INNKEEPER'S DAUGHTER: They soon arrived at an inn, which seemed to Don Quixote to be a castle. A short distance from it he reined in Rocinante, since he hoped a dwarf would appear on the battlements, blowing on his trumpet to give notice that a knight approached. But seeing they were slow about it, and Rocinante was in a hurry to reach the stable, he made for the inn door where two old whores were standing, though to him they seemed to be two fair damsels taking their ease at the castle gate.

DON QUIXOTE: Believe me, beauteous lady, you are most fortunate to have the opportunity of welcoming me to this castle. Not that I shall praise myself, because self-praise is demeaning, but my squire will tell you who I am.

*She laughs at him.*

Moderation is becoming in beautiful maidens, but laughter for no reason, is foolishness.

SANCHO PANZA: So, what do you have for supper, Innkeeper?

INNKEEPER: Whatever you desire! My inn is stocked with birds of the air, fowl of the earth and fish of the sea.

SANCHO PANZA: We have simple tastes, a roast chicken will do us fine.

INNKEEPER: The chicken's off, the hawks ate them all.

SANCHO PANZA: Roast pullets then.

INNKEEPER: I sent fifty pullets off to market only yesterday. Apart from pullets and chicken you can have whatever you desire.

SANCHO PANZA: Veal?

INNKEEPER: No.

SANCHO PANZA: Goat?

INNKEEPER: No.

SANCHO PANZA: Bacon and eggs?

INNKEEPER: Would you leave the chickens out of it? I have no chickens!

SANCHO PANZA: What do you have then?

INNKEEPER: Two lovely cow's shinbones which taste nearly as good as cow's feet boiled in water.

SANCHO PANZA: Right, they're ours. Don't let anyone else eat them.

*They are served their meal.*

INNKEEPER: I see your worship is some class of a knight like in the books. I've got two or three of them books here. When it's harvest time, the reapers stay here, and there's always one of them who can read and he takes up one of these books, and we gather round him, thirty or more of us, and stay listening to him with a delight that makes our grey hairs young again.

MARITORNES: And I like listening to them too, they're so romantic; like when they describe some lady in the arms of her knight under the orange trees, and the old spinster keeping watch for them half dead with the excitement and fright.

DON QUIXOTE: And how do you find them, fair maiden?

INNKEEPER'S DAUGHTER: I don't know indeed, sir, I don't know if I understand them. But I do like listening to them, not for the fights like my father, but the laments of the knights when they're separated from their ladies. Sometimes they make me feel so sad I want to cry.

INNKEEPER'S WIFE: Hush daughter, you know too much about these things.

DON QUIXOTE: Well then, bring me these books, castle-warden, and I shall test the mettle of your library.

*DON QUIXOTE opens a book. Enter THE CAPTIVE.*

THE CAPTIVE: ...I shall therefore tell who I am; I took part in that glorious battle of Lepanto, promoted by this time to Captain of Infantry. But that day, so fortunate for Christendom, was not so fortunate for me. El Uchali, the King of Algiers, a daring corsair, attacked and took the Maltese galley on which I and my company were sailing. Only three of us were left alive, and we were badly wounded. But El Uchali passed me along to a Venetian renegade named Azan Aga and he was very rich. I went with him from Constantinople to Algiers where I hoped to write to Spain and have my ransom paid. But when I arrived, they put chains on me and condemned me to the cells with several other gentlemen. Every day they hanged one man, impaled another, and cut the ears off yet another; all with little provocation or indeed without any. The only one that fared at all well was a Spanish soldier named Miguel de Cervantes. Many times he tried to escape, but his master never laid a finger on him, and only that time does not allow, I could tell you now some of the things Cervantes did, that would astonish you much more than the narration of my own tale.

INNKEEPER: That night they slept in the attic. It had previously been a hayloft. They shared their accommodation with a mule-driver.

MARITORNES: And the mule-driver and myself had arranged to meet for a secret tickle, so to speak, later that night. I told him that when everyone was asleep, I'd come to him and satisfy him in any way he asked.

MULE-DRIVER: So, after I'd given my mules a second ration of feed, I lay down and waited for Maritornes.

SANCHO PANZA: I was already in bed fast asleep, but my master's eyes were as wide open as a hare's.

INNKEEPER'S WIFE: All the inn was silent and the only light came from a lamp hanging in the front door.

CIDE HAMETE BENENGELI: In the marvellous silence, Don Quixote still imagined himself in a famous castle –

INNKEEPER'S DAUGHTER: And that I was the daughter of the lord of the castle, and that I was in love with him and had promised to steal away from my parents that night to be with him –

CIDE HAMETE BENENGELI: And he started to think that his virtue might be compromised. And he resolved not to betray his lady Dulcinea even if Queen Guinevere herself should come to him.

MULE-DRIVER: At the agreed hour, Maritornes, in her nightdress and bare feet, entered the room where the three of us were –

MARITORNES: But as soon as I walked through the door, Don Quixote heard me and sat up in his bed and held out his arms.

DON QUIXOTE: Would that I found myself, exalted lady, in a position to repay the favour you have granted me; but fortune, which never tires of pursuing the virtuous, makes that an impossibility. I have pledged myself to the peerless Dulcinea del Toboso, sole lady of my thoughts; if this did not stand in the way I should not be so insensible a knight as to miss the great opportunity your kindness offers me.

CIDE HAMETE BENENGELI: Maritornes, finding herself in Don Quixote's grasp, attempted to break free. The mule-driver having heard the preceding went to the bed and hit Don Quixote hard in the mouth. Then he jumped on him and trampled on him from head to foot.

INNKEEPER: Where are you, you whore? I know this is your fault.

CIDE HAMETE BENENGELI: Meanwhile Maritornes managed to wrench herself free from Don Quixote's grasp, only to fall backwards over Sancho's bed. Sancho awoke and threw punches in every direction, one of which hit Maritornes who responded in kind. By the light of the innkeeper's lamp, the mule-driver saw this and went to beat Sancho. In the scrum the innkeeper's candle was blown out.

*Darkness.*

OFFICER: Stop in the name of the Holy Brotherhood!

*The OFFICER discovers the bloody DON QUIXOTE.*

In the name of the Holy Brotherhood lock the door of the inn! Make sure no one leaves. A man's been murdered here.

*They all stop fighting.*

ALL: Light. We need light.

*Exit OFFICER. Only SANCHO PANZA and DON QUIXOTE remain.*

DON QUIXOTE: Sancho, my friend, are you asleep?

SANCHO PANZA: How can I sleep when all the devils of hell have beaten me tonight?

DON QUIXOTE: I do believe this castle is enchanted. The daughter of the lord came to me. She was the most beautiful maiden in all the world. And I was engaged in the sweetest of discourse with her, when, without my seeing it, a hand attached to the arm of some giant planted such a fist on my jaw that it's bathed my face in blood. I believe some enchanted Moor is guarding the treasure of this maiden's beauty.

SANCHO PANZA: Well, I feel as though four hundred Moors have beaten me. Bad luck to me and the mother who bore me. I'm no knight-errant and yet I get the worst of it every time.

DON QUIXOTE: True, but you should try to ignore such enchantments, for these beings are invisible and magical so we'll not find anyone on whom to take our revenge. Now get up and saddle Rocinante, Sancho, we need to be ready to leave by sunrise.

INNKEEPER: Leaving already, Sir Knight? What about the bill?

DON QUIXOTE: The bill?

INNKEEPER: The bill. Straw and feed for your animals? Your dinner and beds?

DON QUIXOTE: Then this is an inn?

INNKEEPER: And a fairly good one at that.

DON QUIXOTE: Then you must excuse me, I thought it was a castle, and not a bad one at that.

INNKEEPER: Well it's not, so pay your bill.

DON QUIXOTE: I'm afraid you'll have to excuse me payment, I cannot contravene the rules of knight-errantry. You'll know from your books that knights never pay for lodging or anything else. All hospitality offered them is their due in return for the insufferable toil they endure in seeking adventures by night and by day, in summer and in winter, on foot and on horseback, in hunger and thirst, cold and heat.

INNKEEPER: To hell with your talk of knights and chivalry, pay me what you owe me.

DON QUIXOTE: You are an arsefuck of an innkeeper!

*DON QUIXOTE is gone. The INNKEEPER turns to SANCHO PANZA.*

SANCHO PANZA: What's true for the master is true for the servant.

*SANCHO PANZA is beaten by the INNKEEPER and his guests.*

*DON QUIXOTE returns to help the stricken SANCHO PANZA.*

DON QUIXOTE: I've come to the conclusion, Sancho, that this castle or inn is without doubt enchanted. What else could those who made such vicious sport of you be but phantoms from another world? I swear if I'd been able to I'd have avenged you so violently they'd have remembered it for ever.

SANCHO PANZA: I would have avenged myself too if I could, but I couldn't, because I'm sure they weren't phantoms but men of flesh and bone like ourselves.

*Enter a GUARD leading a PRISONER.*

Don Quixote sir, there's a prisoner up ahead on his way to the galleys under force of the king's men.

DON QUIXOTE: But the king does not use force against anyone.

SANCHO PANZA: I mean he's condemned for his crimes to serve in the king's galleys.

DON QUIXOTE: Are you saying, Sancho, that this man does not go where he is going of his own free will?

SANCHO PANZA: I am.

DON QUIXOTE: Well, if that's the case, I must exercise my office, to succour the needy and help the wretched.

SANCHO PANZA: But he's under the king's orders, your worship, he's being punished for his crimes.

DON QUIXOTE: Tell me, sir, why is this man being transported like this?

GUARD: He's off to the galley as a slave, that's all I know.

DON QUIXOTE: That's as may be, but I'd like to know why.

GUARD: This is no time to discuss his sentence.

*The GUARD tries to go, but the PRISONER tugs him back.*

GINES DE PASAMONTE: I, sir, am like the canary, convicted for singing.

DON QUIXOTE: Are people now sent to the galleys for singing?

GINES DE PASAMONTE: Sir, to sing under suffering means with the criminal fraternity to confess under torture. And 'yes' has less letters than 'never'. Off to the galleys for four years for singing. And pimping. And suspicion of sorcery.

DON QUIXOTE: Apart from the last, you'd hardly deserve such a sentence. Indeed, the office of pimp is no ordinary one, being the office of persons of discretion. It should only be exercised by people of good breeding.

GUARD: Aye, and they should have their own guild too.

DON QUIXOTE: Exactly, like bankers and brokers. But tell me, guard, why is he chained up like this.

GINES DE PASAMONTE: Because he's afraid I'll escape.

GUARD: Don't be listening to him. His list of crimes is as long as my arm. He's got ten years. Might as well be death. His name's Gines de Pasamonte. We call him Don Pissmotherfucker!

GINES DE PASAMONTE: Sir, you were not given your staff of office so you might abuse poor wretches like me, but simply to lead me wherever his Majesty commands you.

DON QUIXOTE: From what you've told me, while you confess to your crimes, you do not see the penalties as just. I'd therefore ask your guard if he'd be so good as to unchain you. It's cruel to make slaves of those God has by nature made free.

GUARD: Get out of here, Sir Prickhead! You don't want to go stirring up a bag of cats.

DON QUIXOTE: And you, sir, are the cat, the rat and the scoundrel!

*DON QUIXOTE charges the GUARD. GINES is freed.*

SANCHO PANZA: But your worship, if he tells the Holy Brotherhood what we've done, they'll come looking for us.

We should go hide in the mountains. The Sierra Morena's not far.

DON QUIXOTE: That's as may be, Sancho, but first I must do something. (*Shouting to the fleeing GINES.*) Sir, high-born people are grateful when they are granted boons. Therefore, in gratitude for the boon I have granted you, I ask you to go at once to the city of El Toboso, and there present yourself to the lady Dulcinea del Toboso.

GINES DE PASAMONTE: I'm afraid what you demand of me, my lord and deliverer, is impossible. I cannot travel the roads openly. The Holy Brotherhood would capture me.

DON QUIXOTE: Then I swear, Don Son-of-a-Whore, Don Pissmotherfucker, or whatever your name is, you will go with your tail between your legs.

*GINES flees. DON QUIXOTE and SANCHO PANZA are afraid because they see a cart approaching, driven by a hideous demon. On the cart is Death, next to it is an angel with large painted wings, a queen, and at one side an emperor, with a crown on his head. At the feet of Death is Cupid with his bow, quiver, and arrows. There is also a knight in full armour.*

Coachman, or is it devil, tell me what you are?

SANCHO PANZA: It would be madness to try to take them on, your worship. An army with Death in its ranks, not to mention emperors and angels.

THE DEVIL: Sir, we are actors from Wing and a Prayer Theatre Company. We were performing the play 'Chariot of Death' this morning in a village behind that hill, and this afternoon we've to do it again in that village there. Since it's so near, and to save time, we're going in costume. That lad there's Death, the other an angel, that woman, the manager's wife, plays the queen, this one the soldier, that the emperor, and I play the Devil, since I'm founder of this company and take all the leading parts.

DON QUIXOTE: By God, when I first saw you I imagined some great adventure was presenting itself, but now I see one 'must touch with the hand what appears to the eye, if illusions are to be avoided'. God speed, good people and break a leg. And, if ever you wish to ask a boon of me, I will do it gladly, for I've been fond of the theatre since I was a boy. In my youth I was a keen student of the actor's art.

*Exit ACTORS.*

The same thing happens in theatre as in life, Sancho, some play emperors, others popes, all the characters of a play. But when it's over, when life ends, death strips us all of the garments that distinguish us from one another. We are all equal in the grave.

SANCHO PANZA: A good comparison, your worship, though I've heard it before. Like that one about the chess game, how when the game's being played, each piece has its special job, but when the game's over they're all mixed and jumbled and shaken together, and stowed away in the bag, like life ends in the grave.

DON QUIXOTE: You're growing less stupid every day, Sancho.

SANCHO PANZA: Perhaps some of your worship's cleverness has stuck to me, but we should be moving or the air'll soon be buzzing with the arrows of the Holy Brotherhood.

## THE SIERRA MORENA

*A small suitcase. SANCHO PANZA looks inside the case and finds a book and some money.*

SANCHO PANZA: Glory be for sending a profitable adventure at last!

DON QUIXOTE: This must belong to some traveller who lost his way in the mountains and was set upon by bandits who killed him and then brought his body to this remote place to bury him.

SANCHO PANZA: But if they were bandits, why would they leave the money?

DON QUIXOTE: In that case…I've no idea how this came to be here. (*Opening the book.*) It seems to be a letter.

SANCHO PANZA: What kind of letter?

DON QUIXOTE: A love letter.

SANCHO PANZA: Read it out, I love love stories.

DON QUIXOTE: (*Reading.*) 'Ungrateful one, you have rejected me for one more wealthy, but not more worthy. By your beauty

I believed you to be an angel, by your deeds I know you are a woman…'

CARDENIO: (*Shouted, off.*) False Fernando! You shall pay.

SANCHO PANZA: Don Quixote, sir, please let me leave, I want to go back to my house and my wife and my children.

DON QUIXOTE: As you wish, Sancho, but I want you to bring report to my lady Dulcinea of all you witness me doing for her. For now I must throw off my armour, tear at my clothes and hit my head on these rocks, along with many other things which shall astonish you.

SANCHO PANZA: For the love of God, if you're going to hit your head, hit it on something soft like water or cotton. I can always tell her ladyship it was a rock.

CARDENIO: (*Shouted, off.*) False Fernando! You shall pay, you shall pay!

SANCHO PANZA: Then let me go to your lady immediately because now I'll have to come back to release you from this purgatory.

DON QUIXOTE: Listen carefully then, because you must commit my letter to memory. 'Sovereign and exalted Lady, he whose heart is pierced by his absence from you, sends you, sweetest Dulcinea del Toboso, the health that he himself does not enjoy. My good squire Sancho will relate to you in full, fairest ingrate, dearest enemy, the condition to which I am reduced on your account. If it be your pleasure to give me relief, I'm yours; if not, do as you please; for by ending my life I shall satisfy your cruelty and my desire. Yours till death, Knight of the Sad Countenance.'

SANCHO PANZA: On my father's life, that's the finest thing I ever heard. I think I'll leave right away without having to watch all the insane things you plan doing.

DON QUIXOTE: But I want you to see me naked, Sancho, performing at least one or two dozen mad acts.

SANCHO PANZA: For the love of God, don't let me see your worship naked. That will make me feel so sad I'll want to cry. If I really must see some insane deeds, please do them fully dressed.

DON QUIXOTE: Have I not said, Sancho, you must wait. It'll be done in a pater noster.

*DON QUIXOTE pulls off his breeches and then turns two cartwheels.*
*SANCHO PANZA departs. Enter CARDENIO.*

I beg you, sir, tell me who you are and what has led you to live your life, like a wild animal, in such a desolate place?

CARDENIO: My name is Cardenio, I was born in one of the finest cities of Andalucia, and in that same city there was a little bit of heaven. Luscinda. I loved her and she loved me. The songs and sonnets I composed about her! But disaster befell me in the guise a friend: Don Fernando, a handsome young gentleman –

FERNANDO: And since there can be no secrets between friends, especially where love is concerned, I soon came to know of Luscinda –

CARDENIO: And he desired to see this rare beauty, and foolishly I yielded to his desire, showing her to him one night by the light of a taper at a grille where we used to whisper to one another –

FERNANDO: I caught a glimpse of her in her dressing gown, and in that moment she drove all thought of other beauties clean out of my thoughts. So delicate, so modest, so tender –

CARDENIO: I felt uneasy to hear such praises coming from his mouth –

FERNANDO: There was no minute of the day I did not want to talk of her –

CARDENIO: He always contrived to read the letters I sent to her, and he had me read him her replies, saying he enjoyed the wit of them. Then, one day, Luscinda returned a book she'd borrowed from me, *Amadis of Gaul,* she was very fond of books of chivalry –

DON QUIXOTE: Had you told me that at the outset, there'd have been no further need to describe her superiority.

LUSCINDA: And in that book I hid a letter. I wrote: 'If you wish to relieve me of the hardship of desiring you but not having you, you may easily do so. My father loves me dearly, and knows you, and I'm sure he'll grant what you might ask him, if you still hold me in the same sentiments that you said you did. L.'

CARDENIO: Unfortunately I confided to Fernando that I dared not approach her father.

FERNANDO: So I told him that I'd talk to Luscinda's father.

CARDENIO: Oh, ambitious Marius! Oh, cruel Catiline! Oh, wicked Sylla! Oh, perfidious Ganelon! Oh, treacherous Vellido! Oh, vindictive Julian! Oh, covetous Judas! Traitor, cruel, vindictive, and perfidious.

### THE ROAD FROM THE SIERRA MORENA

PRIEST: Good God, if that isn't Sancho Panza? And he's riding the horse of my good friend Don Quixote. (*Calling to SANCHO PANZA.*) Sancho Panza, my friend, where is your master? Tell me quick, or I might think you've killed him.

SANCHO PANZA: No need to threaten me, Father, I'm not the kind of man who robs or kills. My master is naked and beating himself up in those mountains, as happy as the day is long. And I am going to Dulcinea, with a letter he ordered me deliver to her. But I must find someone to put it down on paper as soon as possible or I'll forget it completely.

PRIEST: Recite it to me, I have a most elegant hand.

SANCHO PANZA: By God, your reverence, how did it begin? 'High and slobbering lady'.

PRIEST: It wouldn't say 'slobbering', it would say 'supreme' or 'sovereign'.

SANCHO PANZA: That's it, 'sovereign'. Then it said: 'The ignorant sleepless and sore wounded man kisses the hands of your ladyship, ungrateful and unrecognisable beauty.' And then something about health and sickness he was sending her and then it just went along until it ended with 'yours until death, Knight of the Sad Countenance'. You must write it down, your worship.

PRIEST: What must be done is to release your master from that pointless penance in which you say he's engaged.

## THE SIERRA MORENA

CARDENIO: And so, a few days later, I received a letter from Luscinda which read:

LUSCINDA: Don Fernando's undertaking to my father has been carried out more to his benefit than yours. He's asked for my hand, and my father's agreed. The wedding's in two days.

CARDENIO: Now I understood Fernando's generous offer to me. Furious, I went to Luscinda. In secret I entered her house. I was lucky to find her at the same grille that had been witness to our love.

LUSCINDA: Cardenio, I am in my bridal dress, and Don Fernando waits for me in the hall with the other witnesses. They shall witness my death before they witness my agreement. I've a dagger concealed with which I'll put an end to my life.

FERNANDO: (*Off.*) Luscinda! Do you intend keeping me waiting all day?

CARDENIO: Now the night of my sorrow set in, I felt my eyes bereft of light, my mind of reason. I concealed myself behind two tapestries.

FERNANDO: Luscinda!

LUSCINDA: I came out from an antechamber.

CARDENIO: She was the perfection of beauty and elegance. Why do you tantalise me? The priest entered.

DON QUIXOTE: Will you, Lady Luscinda, take Don Fernando as your lawful husband?

CARDENIO: I listened with eager ears and throbbing heart for Luscinda's answer.

LUSCINDA: I do.

CARDENIO: Don Fernando said the same, and giving her the ring they stood joined by a knot that could never be undone.

FERNANDO: I embraced my bride; and she, pressing her hand upon her heart, fainted and fell into her mother's arms.

CARDENIO: I burnt with rage and jealousy. I left the house and the city. By dawn I'd reached these mountains where I intended to end my life.

## THE ROAD FROM THE SIERRA MORENA

PRIEST: I have it, Sancho!

SANCHO PANZA: What?

PRIEST: The perfect plan to lure Don Quixote down from the
mountain. I'll dress myself as a young maiden, and we'll go
to the place where he's doing penance and I'll pretend to be
in some distress or other and ask him a boon which he, as a
knight-errant, shall be bound to grant.

SANCHO PANZA: What's the boon?

PRIEST: That boon shall be to follow me to some place where he
must do battle with an evil knight or somesuch, but really I'll
lead him home.

## THE SIERRA MORENA

DOROTEA: O God, let this be the place that can serve as a tomb
for the burden of this body!

DON QUIXOTE: Stop, your ladyship, whoever you may be, there
is no need to flee. Tell us what has led you to such a wild and
desolate place.

DOROTEA: Love, what else? My life was so cloistered I might
as well have grown up in a convent. But the eyes of love, or
rather lust, are sharper than those of a lynx. They saw me.
His eyes. The eyes of the young duke Don Fernando.

CARDENIO: Oh, ambitious Marius! Oh, cruel Catiline! Oh,
wicked Sylla! Oh, perfidious Ganelon! Oh, treacherous
Vellido! Oh, vindictive Julian! Oh, covetous Judas! Traitor,
cruel, vindictive, and perfidious.

DOROTEA: No sooner had he seen me than he was struck with
love.

FERNANDO: And all her evasions served only to inflame my
appetite.

DOROTEA: Then, one night, as I was in my chamber with the
doors carefully locked lest my honour be endangered
through any carelessness… I know not how it happened, but
I found him standing before me. I did not have the strength
to cry out. My mouth went dry. And he began to say such
things that I, poor child that I was, began, I don't know how,

to think what he said true. I will not yield to any but my lawful husband, I told him.

FERNANDO: If that's your only fear, Dorotea, I give you my word, as heaven is my witness, I'm yours forever.

DOROTEA: Be careful what you swear to, it's just lust talking.

FERNANDO: Let a thousand curses fall on me if I fail to keep this promise. Let me hold you tighter in my arms.

DOROTEA: And after my maid left the room, so did my maidenhead. And so did Don Fernando, as soon as he'd got what he wanted.

FERNANDO: She told me as we parted, that since she was now mine, I might see her other nights in the same way.

DOROTEA: But he did not come again. Then I heard that he'd been married in a neighbouring city to a woman of rare beauty, Luscinda.

CARDENIO: Oh, ambitious Marius! Oh, cruel Catiline! Oh, wicked Sylla! Oh, perfidious Ganelon! Oh, treacherous Vellido! Oh, vindictive Julian! Oh, covetous Judas! Traitor, cruel, vindictive, and perfidious.

## THE ROAD FROM THE SIERRA MORENA

*Enter PRIEST dressed as a princess.*

PRIEST: I fear it might be considered indecent for a priest to dress like this, Sancho.

SANCHO PANZA: Like what?

PRIEST: Like the Princess Micomicona, heiress of the great kingdom of Micomicon, who has come in search of your master to beg a boon of him. That's who.

SANCHO PANZA: But what exactly is the boon?

PRIEST: That he redress a wrong a wicked giant has done me.

SANCHO PANZA: How is that a bad thing? It is good for you and good for me! Especially if my master rights the wrong, and kills that evil-doing giant. But one thing, I beg you, is that you advise him to marry you right away, so he gets his empire and me my island.

PRIEST: I will do everything in my powers to bring this marriage about.

## THE SIERRA MORENA

LUSCINDA: As soon as I said 'I do', I collapsed in a fainting fit. And when the bridegroom unlaced the bosom of my dress to give me air, he found a paper in my handwriting, which said that if I'd accepted Don Fernando, it was only in obedience to my parents. The letter also said that I meant to kill myself on the completion of the marriage.

DOROTEA: On seeing this, Fernando believed it was Luscinda who'd cheated him. He tried to stab her with the dagger he'd found.

CARDENIO: Oh, ambitious Marius –

FERNANDO: Oh shut up!

DOROTEA: But those present restrained him. And after that, I learnt that the door was not yet entirely shut on me.

CARDENIO: So you are the beautiful Dorotea, only child of Clenardo?

DOROTEA: And who are you? And how do you know my name?

CARDENIO: I, good lady, am the unfortunate man who, as you told us, Luscinda declared to be her husband.

DOROTEA: You are Cardenio? Ragged and naked?

CARDENIO: What's worse, I've lost my reason. Except for the odd moments of respite heaven grants me.

DOROTEA: And I'm Dorotea who came to this place to end my life.

DON QUIXOTE: I shall therefore use the prerogative I have as a knight to challenge this Don Fernando, and right the wrongs he has done you. Nor shall I relent until I see you in the arms of Don Fernando and you in the arms of Luscinda.

*Enter masked figures.*

Tell me who goes here or I shall reveal your face with my sword?

FERNANDO: We are very important people on our way to Andalucia. Out of the way.

DON QUIXOTE: And the lady, who is she? I can hear her crying.

FERNANDO: Don't waste your time talking to that woman unless you want to hear lies.

LUSCINDA: I have never told a lie, on the contrary, it's because I'm so truthful I'm now in this miserable state.

CARDENIO: God save us! Whose voice is that?

*The lady loses her veil, revealing her to be LUSCINDA. The man tries to restrain her and loses his mask, revealing him to be DON FERNANDO.*

LUSCINDA: Let me go, Don Fernando, I must convince my husband that I was faithful to him.

FERNANDO: No one move. Luscinda is mine. After the marriage I set out determined to be revenged.

LUSCINDA: He heard I was in a convent, from where he forcibly extracted me.

FERNANDO: And not to now give you up to Cardenio.

DOROTEA: But you must. I lived a happy and honest life until you prised open the doors of my modesty. You cannot belong to Luscinda, because you're mine and she can't be yours, because she belongs to Cardenio. And you pleaded for my virginity, and obtained your desire. Whether you love me or not, I'm your true wife, heaven is my witness.

*FERNANDO releases LUSCINDA from his grip.*

FERNANDO: You win, Dorotea, you win. It's impossible to deny the combined force of so many truths.

*CARDENIO goes to help LUSCINDA.*

CARDENIO: Mistress of my heart, true, constant, and fair.

LUSCINDA: My true master, I am your slave.

*FERNANDO puts his hand on his sword.*

DOROTEA: For God's sake, Don Fernando, let these two lovers live in peace and all shall see that reason has more influence with you than passion.

DON QUIXOTE: I too beg you, sir, to consider Dorotea's tears. You must accept, sir, that it's not by chance we've all met in this improbable place, but by the will of divine providence. Only death should take Luscinda from Cardenio. And, if you consider yourself a Christian and a gentleman, you have no choice but to keep the promise you made her.

FERNANDO: Rise, dear lady, it's not right that what I hold in my heart should be kneeling at my feet. But I beg you one thing: don't reproach me for desiring Luscinda, just look at her now smiling face, and you'll see there an excuse for all my mistakes.

*Enter SANCHO PANZA and the PRIEST, dressed as the Princess Micomicona, who throws himself at the feet of DON QUIXOTE.*

PRIEST: (*As Princess Micomicona.*) From this spot I will not rise, valiant knight, until, by your goodness, you grant a boon to the most distressed damsel under the sun.

DON QUIXOTE: I will not answer a word, beauteous lady, until you rise from the earth.

PRIEST: I will not rise, valiant sir, unless the boon is granted me.

DON QUIXOTE: And I shall grant it provided it may be complied with without detriment or prejudice to my king, my country, or she who holds the key of my heart.

PRIEST: It may be provided without detriment to any of them.

SANCHO PANZA: It's really nothing at all. Only to kill a big giant. And she's the Princess Micomicona, queen of the great kingdom of Micomicon in Ethiopia!

DON QUIXOTE: Be she whosoever she may be. I do only what my knightly conscience bids me.

(*To PRIEST.*) Beauteous lady, rise, for I grant the boon which you ask of me.

PRIEST: What I ask is that your magnanimous personage accompany me, and that you promise to engage in no other adventure or quest until you have avenged me upon the traitor who, against all human and divine law, has usurped my kingdom.

DON QUIXOTE: I repeat that I grant it.

*The PRIEST, still as Princess Micomicona, struggles to kiss the hand of DON QUIXOTE.*

Let us be gone in the name of God to bring aid to this great Princess. Let your highness lead on wheresoever you will.

PRIEST: We must pass right through your village, and there you shall take the road to Cartagena, where you'll be able to leave upon a great ship. And if the wind be fair and the sea smooth, in less than nine years you may come in sight of the great lake of Minges, which is a little over a hundred days' journey from my kingdom.

DON QUIXOTE: Once more, I shall go with you to the end of the earth, if necessary. Though I must make it clear, ma'am, so long as my will is enslaved and my senses enthralled by Dulcinea, it is impossible for me to contemplate marriage, even with a phoenix.

SANCHO PANZA: Are you mad, sir? How can you object to marrying a princess like her? Do you think you'll find such good luck under every stone? Is your Dulcinea prettier? She's not. She's not a patch on this one here. You're looking for sweetmeats in the bottom of the sea, your worship. For the love of God marry her, and take the kingdom that goes with it, then you can make me a marquis or governor of a province at the very least.

DON QUIXOTE: Do you think, you scurvy clown, that you are always free to cause offence and I shall always pardon you? Do you not know, you lout, you vagabond, you beggar, that were it not for the might that Dulcinea lends my arm I'd not have the strength to kill a flea? She fights in me, conquers in me, and I live and breathe in her. I owe my life and being to her. You wretched son of a whore! How ungrateful you are, raised from the dust of the earth to be made a titled lord, and in return you speak evil of her who has bestowed it upon you!

SANCHO PANZA: But Don Quixote, sir, if you don't marry this great princess, the kingdom won't be yours, and if so, how can you reward me? That's why I'm complaining. Why not marry this queen, since she's here, and afterwards go back to your lady Dulcinea. Many's the king who's kept a mistress. As for beauty, let's say I like them both – even though I've never seen the lady Dulcinea.

DON QUIXOTE: Never seen her, doubly blasphemous traitor! Have you not just brought her my letter? Well haven't you?

*DON QUIXOTE beats SANCHO PANZA.*

## THE RETURN HOME

PHANTASMAGORICAL VOICE: O Knight of the Sad Countenance, let not this captivity into which you've been placed upset you. This is necessary for the more speedy accomplishment of the adventure in which you are engaged. It is foretold that it shall be accomplished only when the raging Manchegan lion and the white Tobosan dove are united, having humbled their haughty necks to the gentle yoke of matrimony. And from this marvellous union shall come forth brave whelps that shall rival their valiant father. And as for you, most noble and obedient squire that ever bore a beard upon his face or a nose to smell with, I assure you that your wages shall be paid you,

*They proceed to confine and transport DON QUIXOTE.*

DON QUIXOTE: You, whoever you are, who's foretold me so much good, I beg you ask the enchanter who now persecutes me, that he not leave me to perish in this captivity, at least before I see fulfilled these joyful promises you've just made. Many grave histories of knights-errant have I read, but never yet have I heard of their being carried off in this fashion.

SANCHO PANZA: I don't know what to think, not being as well read as your worship in errant writings, but I don't think these phantoms are quite unknown to us.

DON QUIXOTE: Unknown? Of course they're not unknown to me, they're my enemies.

SANCHO PANZA: (*To those who imprison DON QUIXOTE.*) Do you think I don't understand the reason for these new enchantments? I'm on to you. I know you even if you try to hide your face. Where envy reigns virtue cannot live, as they say. If it weren't for you, my master would be married by now to the Princess Micomicona, the Queen of Micomicon in Ethiopia, and I'd be a count at least.

DON QUIXOTE: Happy the age and happy the time to which the ancients gave the name of golden, not because the gold so coveted in this our age of iron was gained without toil, but because they who lived then knew not the two words 'mine' and 'yours'. In that lucky age all things were in common; to earn your daily food no labour was required but to stretch out your hand and gather it from the sturdy oaks that stood generously inviting you with their sweet ripe fruit. The clear streams and running brooks yielded their cool waters in noble abundance. Fraud, deceit, or malice had then not yet mingled with truth and sincerity. Justice held her ground, unswayed by private interest that now so much perverts her. Maidens and their modesty wandered at will without fear of insult or libertine assault. And if they were undone it was of their own will and pleasure. But now, in this hateful age of ours, no one is safe. And so, in defence of these, as time advanced and wickedness increased, the order of knights-errant was instituted, to defend maidens, protect widows and, in short, succour the needy.

*The confined DON QUIXOTE is led off. CIDE HAMETE BENENGELI remains. Enter SANCHO PANZA.*

SANCHO PANZA: Run! Quick help my master! He's fighting the fiercest battle I've yet seen. He has given the giant, the enemy of my lady the Princess Micomicona, such a slash that he has sliced his head clean off as if it were a turnip.

CIDE HAMETE BENENGELI: Are you in your right senses, Sancho?

SANCHO PANZA: Yes. Why?

CIDE HAMETE BENENGELI: Because how the devil can that be, when we all know that the giant is at least two thousand leagues away?

DON QUIXOTE: (*Off.*) Stand, thief, ruffian, caitiff, villain; now I've got you your scimitar shall not avail you!

SANCHO PANZA: We must go help him – though the giant's surely dead by now. I saw gallons of blood on the ground, and the head cut off and fallen on one side as if it was a large wine-skin.

HOUSEKEEPER: God grant me patience, if Don Quixote or Don Demented has not been slashing some of the skins of red wine that hang above his bed. It's the spilt wine this dog takes for blood.

*End of Act One.*

# Act Two

## THE BOOK

DON QUIXOTE: Tell me Sancho, my friend, what do people think of me? What do they say of my courage, my courtesy, of what I've achieved?

SANCHO PANZA: I'll tell you, on condition you're not angry with me, Don Quixote, sir.

DON QUIXOTE: I promise you, I shall not be angry with you.

SANCHO PANZA: Well then, people consider your worship a mighty great madman, and me no less a fool. As for your worship's courage, courtesy and achievements, there's a variety of opinions. Some say, 'mad but funny'; others, 'courageous but unfortunate'; others, 'courteous but interfering', and then they go into so many witticisms and criticisms of us that they don't leave a pick on our carcasses.

DON QUIXOTE: Remember, Sancho, few famous men have escaped the slander of spiteful tongues. Julius Caesar was charged with being ambitious and not particularly observant in his personal cleanliness.

*Enter CIDE HAMETE BENENGELI as Samson Carrasco.*

CIDE HAMETE BENENGELI: Give me your hands, your highness, Don Quixote de La Mancha, for, by this holy habit, though I've only taken the first four vows, your worship is one of the most famous knights-errant that have ever, or ever will be. A blessing on Cide Hamete Benengeli, who has written the history of your great deeds.

DON QUIXOTE: Can this history be true, Bachelor Carrasco?

CIDE HAMETE BENENGELI: Everything that happened to you is in the book, though how the author could have known so much, I cannot say.

DON QUIXOTE: He must be some wise enchanter. The one thing that gives pleasure to a virtuous and eminent man is to find himself in print in his own lifetime, his good name upon people's lips; I say 'good name', for if it be the opposite, then there is no death so bad.

CIDE HAMETE BENENGELI: In terms of good name, not to mention fame, your worship steals the crown from all other knights-errant.

DON QUIXOTE: And does this author promise a second part?

CIDE HAMETE BENENGELI: He promises one, but says he's not yet found record of further adventures. But, as soon as does, he'll no doubt have it published immediately.

SANCHO PANZA: All I can say is, if my master would take my advice, we'd be back in the field now, redressing outrages and righting wrongs, as a good knight-errant should.

*DON QUIXOTE and SANCHO PANZA prepare to leave.*

HOUSEKEEPER: My master's breaking out, plainly breaking out!

CIDE HAMETE BENENGELI: (*Still as Samson Carrasco.*) What's he breaking out in, housekeeper? The pox?

HOUSEKEEPER: Breaking out of the doors of his sanity, I mean, Bachelor Carrasco. He's off to hunt all over the world for what he calls adventures.

NIECE: That you are so learned, uncle, and yet are so foolish as to think yourself young when you're old, strong when you're sick, a knight when you're not one –

HOUSEKEEPER: You must help us, Bachelor Carrasco.

CIDE HAMETE BENENGELI: How can we help what heaven has determined? O flower of knight-errantry! O shining light of arms! O honour and mirror of the Spanish nation!

HOUSEKEEPER: Damned idiot! Is this your idea of help?

CIDE HAMETE BENENGELI: Blessed be Allah! Blessed be almighty Allah! Three times blessed be almighty Allah! Once more Don Quixote and his faithful squire, Sancho Panza, set forth into the Manchegan countryside, this time taking the road to El Toboso.

## THE ROAD TO EL TOBOSO

DON QUIXOTE: Nothing in life makes knights-errant more valourous than finding themselves favoured by their ladies, Sancho. But night is drawing in and I fear we'll not reach El Toboso by dusk.

SANCHO PANZA: Besides, it will be difficult enough for your worship to receive her blessing, unless she throws it over the wall of the yard where she was working when I took her the letter.

DON QUIXOTE: It must have been the balcony of some fine palace you took for a yard wall, Sancho, and I presume you mean walking not working.

SANCHO PANZA: Well, to tell the truth, your worship, when I saw your luminous lady she was not bright enough to throw out many beams. It must have been because she was sifting wheat and the thick dust she raised clouded her face and stuck to her sweat.

DON QUIXOTE: Why do you still persist, Sancho, in maintaining that my lady Dulcinea was sifting wheat?

*SANCHO PANZA, alone.*

SANCHO PANZA: So, Sancho my friend, where are you going now? Are you off to look for an donkey that's been lost? No, just a princess, that's all. And what kind of princess, Sancho? Just one out of whose backside the sun of beauty and the whole heaven shines. And where do you expect to find such a princess? Why, in the tiny hamlet of El Toboso of course! And who are you looking for this princess for? For the famous knight Don Quixote de La Mancha. And do you know her house, Sancho? My master says it will be some royal palace or grand castle. And have you ever even seen this princess by any chance? Neither I nor my master have ever clapped eyes on her –

*SANCHO PANZA sees two peasant-girl 'DULCINEAS'. He has an idea.*

Queen and princess and duchess of beauty, may it please your haughtiness and heartiness to receive into your favour your captive knight who stands there stupefied and marblised at finding himself in your magnificent presence. I am Sancho Panza, his squire, and he the vagabond knight Don Quixote de La Mancha, otherwise called 'Knight of the Sad Countenance'.

FIRST DULCINEA: Out of the way and let us pass, we're in a hurry.

SANCHO PANZA: Oh, princess of El Toboso, is your big heart not softened by seeing the pillar of knight-errantry on his knees before you?

SECOND DULCINEA: Look at how the gentry are making fun of us peasant girls now.

FIRST DULCINEA: As if we didn't know how to give as good as we get.

SECOND DULCINEA: Out of the way if you don't want a beating.

FIRST DULCINEA: Out of the way or we'll tan your arse.

DON QUIXOTE: I see that fortune has closed all roads by which this wretched soul might find comfort. The evil enchanter who persecutes me has cast cataracts upon my eyes, and to them, and only them, has he transformed the unparalleled beauty of your features into those of an ugly peasant girl. And, no doubt, I appear to you as some sort of a loathsome old monster too. But I beg you do not turn away from my outward appearance.

FIRST DULCINEA: Listen, you dirty old fornicator, leave me alone with your fancy stuff.

SECOND DULCINEA: Yeah, go boil your head.

FIRST DULCINEA: And your arse.

DON QUIXOTE: See how I'm hated by the enchanters! Not content with transforming the appearance of my Dulcinea they also transformed the smell. When I approached her I got such a whiff of raw garlic it made my head spin.

SANCHO PANZA: Oh, scum of the earth! Oh, miserable, spiteful enchanters! They should be strung up by the gills, like sardines on a stick! Was it not enough for you to have changed the pearls of my lady's eyes into crab apples, and her hair of purest gold into the bristles of a red ox's tail, without meddling with her smell? Though I saw no blemish, only purest beauty.

DON QUIXOTE: I believe you, Sancho my friend, though I saw nothing but ugliness!

*They resume their journey.*

One thing does strike me, however. You said her eyes were pearls, but eyes like pearls are more like the eyes of a sea-bream than a lady. I believe Dulcinea's resemble green emeralds, full and soft, with two rainbows for eyebrows. Those pearls belong in her mouth Sancho, for it's clear you've mistaken her eyes for her teeth.

SANCHO PANZA: Yes, that must be it.

## THE CAVE OF MONTESINOS

DON QUIXOTE: What are these lights coming from this hole? Lower me into the abyss, Sancho, for surely this must be the gates of hell.

SANCHO PANZA: Think what you're doing, Don Quixote, sir. You don't want to be left dangling like a jar tied down a well to cool.

DON QUIXOTE: Tie the rope and be quiet, Sancho.

*SANCHO PANZA lowers DON QUIXOTE down into the cave.*

THIRD DULCINEA: O ill-fated Montesinos! O sore-wounded Durandarte! O unhappy Belerma! O tearful Guadiana, and you, O hapless daughters of Ruidera!

*DON QUIXOTE arrives in the cave. Two doors in the palace open and an old man with a long grey beard enters.*

MONTESINOS: For a long time now, O valiant Don Quixote de La Mancha, we who are here enchanted in these solitudes have been hoping you'd come, to make known to you the secrets of the deep cave of Montesinos. For I am the great Montesinos himself.

SANCHO PANZA: If that's the case, and that one's dead, how come he moans and sighs, as if he were still alive?

DURANDARTE: O my cousin Montesinos!
'Twas my last request of you,
That when my soul had left my body,
You do as I'd bid you do,
And with your trusty dagger
Cut the heart out of my breast,
And take it to the fair Belerma.
This was my last request.

MONTESINOS: And I removed your heart, as you asked me, as best I could. And, having laid the rest of you in the earth at Roncesvalles, I took the road to France with your heart – after sprinkling a little salt on it to keep it sweet – and brought it, if not fresh, then at least well cured, to the Lady Belerma. But now I've news for you, cousin: the great knight Don Quixote de La Mancha, of whom the sage Merlin has prophesied such extraordinary things and by whose intervention we shall all be disenchanted, has come.

*A wailing procession of maidens in mourning, the leader of whom, Lady Belerma, carries a heart.*

MONTESINOS: The Lady Belerma. See how she suffers, damned to hold for ever that heart in her hand. Were it not for this affliction, the great Dulcinea del Toboso herself would hardly be a match for her beauty.

SANCHO PANZA: Punch him, sir, and pluck his beard until his chin is bare.

DON QUIXOTE: No, Sancho, we should respect the old, especially if they're enchanted.

SANCHO PANZA: Do the enchanted eat?

DON QUIXOTE: They do not eat, nor excrete, though I believe their nails, beards and hair all continue to grow.

MONTESINOS: The hour's approaching when you must leave the abyss.

THIRD DULCINEA: Dulcinea del Toboso kisses your worship's hands, and would like to know how you are; and, being in great need, she also asks you to be so good as to lend her half a dozen reals, or whatever you have on you. She promises to repay them very soon.

CIDE HAMETE BENENGELI: No. No, I am not convinced that everything that happened in the preceding scene to the valiant Don Quixote could have happened as reported. For instance, if the apparitions appeared solely in Don Quixote's imagination, how could Sancho have seen them. And if they were actual and tangible, who created them? No, all the adventures that have occurred up to the present have, at least, been feasible; but this one of the cave, it stretches believability. Furthermore it is said that at the time of his death Don Quixote confessed he had invented it. Therefore, you must decide for yourselves.

## ON THE RIVER

DON QUIXOTE: What are you afraid of my butter-hearted friend? We must have already travelled seven hundred leagues. If I had here an astrolabe to take the altitude of the North Star, I could tell you exactly how far. We'll shortly cross the equatorial line which stands halfway between the poles.

SANCHO PANZA: And when we reach that line how far shall we have travelled?

DON QUIXOTE: Very, very far, for of the three hundred and sixty degrees that this terraqueous globe contains, as computed by Ptolemy, we'll have travelled one half when we reach the line.

SANCHO PANZA: What, in the name of God, are you talking about, your worship sir?

DON QUIXOTE: And you know, Sancho, from the Spaniards who travel to the East Indies, one of the signs that they've crossed the equatorial line is that the lice die upon everybody on board. Not a single one is left. So, Sancho, put your hand down your breeches, and if you come across anything alive we'll know we're not there yet; if not, then we've crossed it.

SANCHO PANZA: I'll do as you ask, though I don't know what need there is for experiments, since I can see with my own two eyes that we've not moved five yards.

DON QUIXOTE: Do the test, Sancho, and don't mind what your senses might tell you, for you know nothing of parallels, zodiacs, ecliptics, and planets of which the celestial and terrestrial spheres are composed. If you did, you'd know how many parallels we have traversed. But since you don't, hunt in your breeches, I'm sure they'll be cleaner than a sheet of white paper.

*SANCHO PANZA rummages in his breeches and finds a louse.*

SANCHO PANZA: Either the experiment's a failure, or we've not come to where your worship says.

## THE DUKE AND DUCHESS

DON QUIXOTE: Run, Sancho my son, and tell the noble lady that I kiss her beautiful hands. And for once watch how you speak.

SANCHO PANZA: Fair lady, this knight, Knight of the Sad Countenance, is my master, and he greets you, and I am his squire, Sancho Panza.

THE DUCHESS: Is this master of yours not the one about whom there's currently a book, *The Ingenious Gentleman, Don Quixote of La Mancha?*

SANCHO PANZA: The selfsame, your grace, and I'm that same squire.

THE DUCHESS: How delightful! Go, Panza, and tell your master that he is welcome to my estate, indeed, that nothing could give me or my husband, the Duke, greater pleasure.

*DON QUIXOTE goes towards THE DUCHESS but trips and falls.*

THE DUKE: I am saddened, Sir Knight of the Sad Countenance, that your first experience on my estate should have been such an unfortunate one.

DON QUIXOTE: That which has occurred, mighty prince, cannot be unfortunate, for any misfortune is offset by the great fortune of meeting you. However I may be, fallen or raised up, on foot or on horseback, I shall always be at your service and that of my lady the Duchess, your worthy consort and paramount princess of courtesy.

*Dinner. Sitting at the table is an ECCLESIASTIC.*

SANCHO PANZA: If your worships will allow me I'll tell you a story from my village about seating arrangements.

DON QUIXOTE: Your graces would be well advised to have this fool removed from the table, or he'll spout such a heap of nonsense –

THE DUCHESS: Sancho shall not be taken from me for a moment.

SANCHO PANZA: Well, the story I was going to tell was this: there was an invitation given by a gentleman in my village, a very rich man, quality, related to the Alamos of Medina del Campo, and married to the Lady Mencia of Quinones, the daughter of Don Alonso of Maranon, Knight of the Order of Santiago, who was drowned at the Herradura – there was a quarrel about him years ago in our village which my master Don Quixote also got mixed up in too, the one that

Tomasillo the trickster, the son of Balbastro the baker, was wounded in. It's all true, isn't it master? Tell them or they'll think I'm lying.

THE ECCLESIASTIC: So far, you seem more chatterbox than a liar, though I'm keeping an open mind.

DON QUIXOTE: Go on, Sancho, but try to shorten the story.

THE DUCHESS: He's not to cut it short, even if it takes six days.

SANCHO PANZA: Well then, sirs, I was saying, that this gentleman, of quality, the Alamos of Medina and all that, whom I know as well as my own hands, for it's not a stone's throw from my house to his, invited a poor but respectable labourer –

THE ECCLESIASTIC: At this rate you'll still be telling it in the next world.

SANCHO PANZA: So this labourer, coming to the house of the gentleman that invited him – God rest his soul for he's now dead – though he died the death of an angel, so they say, for I wasn't there, because I'd gone for the harvest at Tembleque –

DON QUIXOTE: Sancho, please come back from Tembleque, and finish your story.

SANCHO PANZA: Well then, as the pair of them were about to sit down to table – I can see them now clear as day – the labourer insisted the gentleman take the head of the table, and the gentleman insisted the labourer take it. But the labourer, who prided himself on his good manners, would on no account take the place at the head of the table, until the gentleman, out of patience, put his hands on the labourer's shoulders, and forced him to sit down, saying, 'Sit down, you stupid fool, because wherever I sit will be the head of the table to you.'

THE DUCHESS: I was wondering, Don Quixote sir, what news have you of the lady Dulcinea? Have you sent her any giants or malefactors recently?

DON QUIXOTE: Your grace, my misfortunes, though they had a beginning, shall never have an end. For how are those I defeat or succour meant to find her when she's enchanted, turned into the most unpleasant peasant wench imaginable?

SANCHO PANZA: And yet to me she seemed the fairest creature in the world.

THE ECCLESIASTIC: This Don Quixote, or Don Crackpot, or whatever his name is, cannot, I'm sure, be such a fool as your grace believes him to be, encouraging him to continue with his vagaries and follies. And as for you, you idiot, you should go home and bring up your children, if you have any, and attend to your business, and stop making a laughing-stock of yourself to all and sundry.

DON QUIXOTE: The presence in which I stand, and the respect I have and always have had for the Church bind the hands of my indignation. Also, because I know that a clergyman's weapon is the same as a woman's, i.e. the tongue, I will therefore use mine to engage in equal combat with that of your excellency. Let me say just this by way of parry and riposte: you accuse me of vagaries and follies, yet are not my intentions always directed towards worthy ends, they being to do good to all and evil to none? And if he who means this, does this, and makes this his practice, if he deserves to be called a fool, surely it is for our hosts, your graces, most excellent duke and duchess, to determine.

SANCHO PANZA: Touché, master, your thrust has hit home as they say.

THE ECCLESIASTIC: And you must be that Sancho Panza to whom your master has promised an island?

SANCHO PANZA: That's me, and there'll be no lack of empires for him to rule or islands for me to govern.

THE DUKE: No, Sancho my friend, you're right, for in the name of Don Quixote de La Mancha, I'll confer on you the government of an island of no small importance that I have on my estate.

DON QUIXOTE: Go down on your knees, Sancho. Kiss the feet of his grace.

THE ECCLESIASTIC: By the gown I wear, I'm almost inclined to say that your grace is as great a fool as these sinners. No wonder they are mad, when people who are in their senses sanction their madness! I'll leave you to them, for so long as they are in the house, I shall remain in my own.

*Exit* ECCLESIASTIC.

*The sound of a battle cry is heard; trumpets, bugles, drums, fifes.*
*All fall silent. A* DEMON *passes in front of them.*

DEMON: I am a devil and I'm looking for Don Quixote de La
Mancha.

THE DUKE: And who are they?

DEMON: Those are the six regiments of enchanters, carrying on
a triumphal cart the peerless Dulcinea del Toboso.

DON QUIXOTE: If you were the Devil, as you claim, you would
have known Don Quixote de La Mancha, for I am he.

DEMON: By God and upon my conscience, I didn't recognise
you.

SANCHO PANZA: This devil's a good Christian, swearing by God
and his conscience.

*The* DEMON *sounds his horn and exits.*

THE DUKE: Does your worship intend to stay here?

DON QUIXOTE: How could I not when these enchanters hold my
Dulcinea captive? I'll stand fast even if all hell attacks me.

*The sound of an approaching oxcart is heard. On the cart sits*
*an old man, his beard whiter than snow.*

MERLIN: I am Merlin whom the histories tell
Had for his father the Devil himself,
Down in the deathly caverns of Dis
Where my soul dwells the far side of the Styx;
There came complaint in a voice that I know,
That of the Dulcinea del Toboso.
It told of her enchantment and of her fate,
Transformed from lady into peasant state.
And so touched with pity by her vile looks
I went and consulted my special books,
My books of black magic and alchemy,
In order to find fitting remedy.
And so, knight, never sufficiently praised,
Star of La Mancha, to you I now say:
For Dulcinea to regain her true form
Sancho Panza, your squire, must bare and turn
His ample buttocks up towards the sky

And lash them three thousand three hundred times
Until they be red and raw and wretched,
So shall Dulcinea be disenchanted.

SANCHO PANZA: To hell with such ways of disenchantment! I
don't see what my backside's got to do with anything. Let
Lady Dulcinea go to her grave enchanted for all I care.

DON QUIXOTE: Then I'll take you, you garlic-munching gibbon,
and tie you to a tree, and strip you as naked as when your
mother brought you into this world, and give you six
thousand six hundred lashes.

MERLIN: That won't do, Sancho's lashes must be received by his
own free will, not by force.

SANCHO PANZA: Not a hand, my own or anybody else's, shall
touch me. He's the one who ought to whip himself. But me?
Never!

FOURTH DULCINEA: Wicked squire! Soul of a beer jug and
heart of a cork tree! If we'd asked you to throw yourself off
some tall tower, or eat a dozen toads, or kill your children,
then such objections would be understandable. But to make
a fuss about three thousand three hundred lashes? What
every poorhouse boy gets each month! Turn your frightened
rabbit's eyes to mine, Sancho, mine that have been
compared to radiant stars, liberate the softness of my flesh,
Sancho, the ampleness of my figure. And if not for my sake,
then do it for that poor knight whose soul I can this moment
see stuck in his throat.

DON QUIXOTE: By God, what Dulcinea says is true, my soul is
stuck in my throat, like the nut of a crossbow.

THE DUCHESS: What do you say to this, Sancho?

SANCHO PANZA: I say where did this lady Dulcinea del Toboso,
learn how to ask favours? She comes to ask me to flay my
flesh with lashes, and then calls me 'soul of a beer jug'?
Is my flesh brass? Besides, what is it to me whether she is
enchanted or not?

## THE BEDCHAMBER

ALTISADORA: (*Off or from darkness.*) Urge me not to sing, you
demons of the night. You know that ever since I first set eyes

upon this stranger, I cannot sing but only weep. Besides if her grace finds us here –

DEMON: Do not worry, Altisadora, if the Duchess hears she'll blame it on the hot night.

ALTISADORA: That's not what I fear, demons, it's that I fear my singing shall betray my true feelings, and I be thought a wanton harlot. But I must sing, I cannot help myself.

*ALTISADORA sings. DON QUIXOTE is amazed by what he hears.*

DON QUIXOTE: What a knight of so many misfortunes am I that any woman who sets eyes on me cannot help but fall in love with me! Why do you pursue me, you empresses? Why do you persecute me, you princesses? What do you want from me, you fourteen- and fifteen-year-old virgins? For me Dulcinea alone is beautiful, wise, virtuous, graceful, and well bred. All others are ill-favoured, foolish, light, and low born. So leave me in peace, I beg you.

*A sack of cats is lowered from the ceiling. To DON QUIXOTE they are a legion of devils.*

Away evil enchanters! Wicked wizards! For I am Don Quixote de La Mancha.

*One cat jumps onto his face and sinks its claws into him. He grapples with it around the room.*

No one is to pull him away. Let me fight hand-to-hand with this demon, this wizard, this enchanter, I'll teach him Don Quixote de La Mancha is not to be trifled with.

## THE PUBLIC GALLERY

THE DUKE: Since your worship has so little time with us, many of the afflicted have come from all parts to seek you out.

*Enter the COUNTESS TRIFALDI. She kneels down.*

COUNTESS TRIFALDI: Are you the most unblemished knight Don Quixote de La Manchissima?

SANCHO PANZA: That's him, and I'm his squire, Sancho Panzissima.

COUNTESS TRIFALDI: At your feet I throw myself, for these legs are the columns which support the temple of knight-errantry. O untainted knight, the enchantment I wish to tell you of is so terrifying that my lady Maguncia, Queen of Candaya, was buried within three days with the shock of its discovery.

SANCHO PANZA: Was she dead?

COUNTESS TRIFALDI: Of course. We don't bury the living even in Candaya. It was on the day of her daughter's marriage to the knight Don Clavijo, there appeared at the church the jealous giant Malambruno. He claimed the girl had been promised to him. He left them there, all enchanted, turning the girl into a brass monkey and Don Clavijo into a crocodile. He then called all the ladies of the palace, those here with me now, and said he would condemn us to a punishment which would be social death. When he stopped speaking we all felt the pores of our faces opening, and pricking us, as if with the points of needles. We put our hands up to our faces and found ourselves in the state you now see.

*The COUNTESS TRIFALDI and her handmaids raise their veils and reveal their various beards.*

What, I ask you, is a lady with a beard to do? What father or mother will feel pity for her? Who will help her? For, even when she has a smooth skin, and a face flayed by a thousand soaps and scrubs and cosmetics, she can't get anybody to love her. What will she do when she has a face like a bush?

SANCHO PANZA: I swear by the ghosts of all my ancestors the Panzas, that I never, in all my born days, never did see or hear of an enchantment as horrible as this.

THE DUCHESS: What about a barber? Can you not have yourselves shaved?

COUNTESS TRIFALDI: We shave twice daily. Some of us have even taken to using bandages soaked in hot wax.

DON QUIXOTE: I will pluck out my own beard in the land of the Moors, if I don't cure your bristling affliction. What must I do, your ladyship?

COUNTESS TRIFALDI: It is five thousand leagues from here to Candaya. But the giant Malambruno told me that, if fate provided the great Don Quixote de La Mancha as our deliverer, he himself would send a horse which flies through the air with such rapidity that you would fancy the Devil himself was carrying him. It will have you there in the wink of a royal eye.

SANCHO PANZA: And how many is there room for on this horse?

COUNTESS TRIFALDI: Two, one in the saddle, one on the rump. O Giant Malambruno, even though you are a wicked enchanter, and a giant, you keep your promises! Send us your horse, the flying Clavileno. Let the knight who has the biggest heart mount this infernal machine!

SANCHO PANZA: Not me then, for I'm no knight and my heart's no bigger than a butter bean.

COUNTESS TRIFALDI: Valiant knight, the horse has arrived, our beards are growing, and by their every hair we beg you to mount him with your squire and begin your new journey.

SANCHO PANZA: Don Quixote, sir, I don't have a big enough heart for this adventure.

DON QUIXOTE: I've never seen Sancho so afraid as now. If I were superstitious, his fear might worry me. Sancho, a word or two to you in private. Listen my friend, what with the long journey before us and the Lord himself not knowing when we'll return, I want you to go to your chamber, as though you were going to fetch something for our journey, and quickly give yourself five hundred lashes of the three thousand three hundred you owe. It will be to the best. To make a start is to be half done, as they say.

SANCHO PANZA: Are you completely mad your worship? Let us be off to shave these ladies. When we return, I'll do the lashes, I promise.

DON QUIXOTE: Well, I must content myself with the promise, my good Sancho, and I believe you shall keep it. For although you're stupid, you are honest.

*They mount Clavileno.*

Cover your eyes, Sancho, and get on.

SANCHO PANZA: Let's be off, your worship. These ladies' beards really do upset me.

*DON QUIXOTE is blindfolded. He spurs the horse. All the women shout.*

BEARDED LADIES: God guide you, valiant knight! God be with you, intrepid squire! Now, now you are shooting through the air like an arrow! You amaze all who are gazing at you from the earth! Take care not to wobble about, brave Sancho! Mind you do not fall, for your fall would be from such a great height.

SANCHO PANZA: Sir, how can they say that we're flying so high, if we can hear their voices.

DON QUIXOTE: Don't mind that, Sancho, for since flights like this are out of the ordinary, why shouldn't one hear things from a thousand leagues off? But please, don't cling to me quite so tightly or you'll unseat me. And really I don't know what you're worried about, for I can safely say I've never ridden such a smooth and steady beast, you'd almost think we'd not moved from the spot.

*Air is blown at them.*

SANCHO PANZA: But the wind on this side's so strong, it's as if people pumped a thousand pairs of bellows at us.

DON QUIXOTE: That means, Sancho, we've reached the second region of the air, whence hail and snow originate. Thunder, lightning and thunderbolts are engendered in the third region, and if we carry on climbing at this rate, we shall soon reach the fourth.

SANCHO PANZA: The fourth? What happens there?

DON QUIXOTE: The region of fire, and I can't steer very well with this steering stick, so I've no way of stopping us being burned.

*Hot coals held up to them.*

SANCHO PANZA: May the Lord have mercy on us! We're already in that fiery region, or very near it, my beard's been singed. I want to look and see where we are, your worship.

DON QUIXOTE: Remember the true story of the novice priest Torralva who the devils carried through the air riding on a stick with his eyes shut? The Devil bid him open his eyes, and he did, and saw himself so near the moon, that he could have reached out and touched it, but he did not dare to look at the earth lest he be seized with giddiness. So, Sancho, do not look.

*To finish, hot coals are placed in the rear of the horse causing fireworks to explode. DON QUIXOTE and SANCHO PANZA fall to the ground having been burned and singed.*

## THE INN

*Enter a puppeteer with a taffeta eyepatch.*

MASTER PEDRO: My host, any room for me and the divining monkey?

(*Monkey voice.*) Good lord, it's Master Pedro the Puppeteer! But where's the monkey, I don't see him.

(*Pedro.*) The monkey's here, and let him come in, because tonight there are people who will pay to see the monkey's talents.

*MASTER PEDRO has a puppet monkey.*

DON QUIXOTE: A divining monkey? Can you tell us what will become of us?

MASTER PEDRO: Sir, I'm afraid this animal does not give information about things to come, but about the past he knows a little, and the present, a little more.

SANCHO PANZA: By God, I wouldn't pay anything to have someone tell me what's already happened to me. Who knows better than me?

DON QUIXOTE: In my opinion his owner must have made a pact with the Devil. Because the monkey only replies to past or present things, which is as far as the Devil's knowledge extends. Future things cannot be known, for knowing all times and moments is reserved to God alone.

MASTER PEDRO: Well then, why don't we read another chapter of the second part of *Don Quixote de La Mancha*.

DON QUIXOTE: The second part? It's written already?

MASTER PEDRO: Yes. While no one who's read the first could like the second so much, and the author, Avellanada, has none of the subtleties of that great historian, Cide Hamete Benengeli. But there's no book so bad that it doesn't have some good in it, as they say. What I don't like in this part is that it shows Don Quixote out of love with Dulcinea.

*DON QUIXOTE is outraged once again. Enter a figure identical to him.*

THE FALSE QUIXOTE: If anyone says that Don Quixote of La Mancha has forgotten or ever can forget Dulcinea del Toboso I shall make him understand with my strong arm that he is very far from the truth, because the peerless Dulcinea cannot be forgotten, nor does forgetting have any place in the character of Don Quixote; constancy is his coat of arms.

MASTER PEDRO: Who said that?

THE FALSE QUIXOTE: Who else but Don Quixote de La Mancha.

MASTER PEDRO: So you are the true Quixote? The polestar, the guiding light of knight-errantry, despite the attempts to usurp your good name by the author of this book?

*MASTER PEDRO and the two DON QUIXOTES read the book together.*

THE FALSE QUIXOTE: Let anyone who wishes portray me, but not mistreat me, for patience is crushed under the weight of insult. Having read it, I can confirm that it is indeed a very foolish sequel. One should eschew obscene and indecent things.

DON QUIXOTE: Tell me, knight, who are you really?

THE FALSE QUIXOTE: I am really Don Quixote de La Mancha, sir knight.

DON QUIXOTE: Then who am I?

THE FALSE QUIXOTE: Who indeed?

DON QUIXOTE: Which way are you travelling, sir?

THE FALSE QUIXOTE: To Zaragoza for the jousting.

MASTER PEDRO: In this sequel you…he…you…they go to the jousting tournament in Zaragoza.

THE FALSE QUIXOTE: Such is the fame that precedes me.

DON QUIXOTE: For that reason, I shall not set foot in Zaragoza. In this way I'll show the falsehood of this sequel to the world and people shall see that I am not this clownish fabrication this false historian describes.

MASTER PEDRO: And there are jousts too in Barcelona. You could go there to prove your valour and prove you are still your own man.

## THE ROAD

*They are alone, lost in the night.*

DON QUIXOTE: What's wrong, Sancho? What's made you so afraid?

SANCHO PANZA: The trees are full of feet and legs.

DON QUIXOTE: You've nothing to be afraid of, the feet and legs belong to outlaws hanged on the trees. The authorities in this region hang them in their twenties and thirties when they catch them. It means that we must be near Barcelona.

## BARCELONA

CIDE HAMETE BENENGELI: By unfrequented roads our heroes made their slow way to Barcelona, reaching there the sea on St John's Eve; night. So it was not till first light that for the first time in their lives Sancho and Quixote saw the sea. It struck them as a thing of greatest beauty, dazzling, broad and infinite, and for what seemed like an age, they gazed at it in silence. Towards noon, horsemen dressed in livery galloped towards them along the strand and shouted to them and cheered them and offered them their hands in welcome...

DON ANTONIO: Welcome to our city, mirror, beacon, star and nonpareil of all knights-errant! Welcome valiant Don Quixote de La Mancha; not the false and fictitious one recently described in deceitful histories, but the true and legitimate one that Cide Hamete Benengeli, flower of historians, has described to us! Come with us, Don Quixote sir, for we are all of us your servants.

DON QUIXOTE: Great are the rewards of knight-errantry, for he who follows the path is known the world over.

DON ANTONIO: Just as fire cannot be hidden, virtue cannot escape being recognised.

## DON ANTONIO'S HOUSE

DON ANTONIO: Now I am going to astound your worship with what you will witness. This head has been crafted by one of the greatest wizards the world has ever seen, a Pole, who was a guest here in my house. For a thousand crowns he constructed this head which can answer any question put to it. Head, tell me what am I thinking at this moment?

HEAD: I cannot construe thoughts.

DON ANTONIO: How many of us are here?

HEAD: You and your wife, with two friends of yours, and two of hers, and a famous knight called Don Quixote de La Mancha, and his squire, Sancho Panza.

DON ANTONIO: This suffices to prove to me that I was not deceived by he who made you. But let someone else put a question to it.

A WOMAN: Tell me, Head, what should I do to be the most beautiful?

HEAD: Mix with the most ugly.

NEXT WOMAN: I'd like to know, Head, whether my husband loves me.

HEAD: Do you really want to know?

GENTLEMAN: Who am I?

HEAD: That is the purpose of the journey.

GENTLEMAN: What journey?

HEAD: You'll know when you reach your destination.

DON QUIXOTE: Tell me, was what I saw in the cave of Montesinos the truth or a dream? And shall Sancho's whipping be accomplished without fail? And shall the disenchantment of Dulcinea ever be achieved?

HEAD: As to the question of the cave, there is much to be said; there is something of both in it. Sancho's whipping will proceed at a leisurely pace. And the disenchantment of Dulcinea will attain its final consummation.

SANCHO PANZA: Head, shall I ever be the governor of an island? Shall I ever escape from the hard life of a squire? Shall I ever get home to see my wife and children?

HEAD: You shall be governor of your own home, and, if each man be an island, you shall therefore have your island. And in returning home to govern, you shall see your wife and children. And on ceasing to serve you shall cease to be a squire.

SANCHO PANZA: I could have told you that myself! Though you put it better.

*Night. The WOMEN want to dance with DON QUIXOTE for a joke. He is an ungainly dancer.*

DON QUIXOTE: Fugite, partes adversae! Leave me in peace; avaunt, with your desires, ladies, for she who is my queen, the peerless Dulcinea del Toboso, suffers none but herself to hold me captive and subdue me.

*He sits in the middle of the floor, broken by the dancing.*

## THE DEFEAT

*A KNIGHT with a white moon painted on his shield rides towards DON QUIXOTE.*

KNIGHT OF THE WHITE MOON: Illustrious knight, Don Quixote de La Mancha, I am the Knight of the White Moon and I've come to do battle with you and make you confess that my lady, Casildea de Vandalia, is incomparably more beautiful than your Dulcinea del Toboso. If you confess this now, you shall escape death and save me the trouble of inflicting defeat upon you. If you fight and I defeat you, I demand no other satisfaction than that, laying aside arms you desist forthwith from going in search of adventures, and return to your own village for a year, in peace and quiet and beneficial repose, being needful, as it is, for the salvation of your soul.

DON QUIXOTE: Knight of the White Moon, whose achievements and whose lady, Casildea de Vandalia, I have never heard of until now. Nevertheless, I will hazard that you have never seen the illustrious Dulcinea; for had you, I know you'd have taken care not to challenge me upon this issue. I do not say you lie, but merely that you are incorrect, so I must accept your challenge. Take whichever side of the field you wish.

*They draw their swords and fight until* DON QUIXOTE *is defeated.*

KNIGHT OF THE WHITE MOON: You're beaten, sir knight, and dead unless you admit what I demanded.

DON QUIXOTE: (*As though speaking from the tomb.*) Dulcinea del Toboso is the fairest woman in the world, and I the most unfortunate knight on earth. It is not right that this truth should suffer due to my human frailty. Drive your lance home, sir knight, and take my life, since you have taken away my honour.

KNIGHT OF THE WHITE MOON: That I will not. I can't. Let the fame of the lady Dulcinea's beauty live undimmed for ever. All I require is that you, Don Quixote, retire to your own home for a year, as agreed.

*The* KNIGHT *raises his visor to reveal that he is* CIDE HAMETE BENEGELI. *He turns and enters the city.* SANCHO PANZA *does not know what to say or do.*

DON ANTONIO: May God forgive you, sir, for the wrong you've done the whole world in trying to bring its most amusing madman back to his senses. Any benefits of Don Quixote's sanity can never equal the joy his madness gave us. In spite of Bachelor Carasco's best efforts might Don Quixote never be cured, for by his recovery not only do we lose his clownings, but his squire Sancho Panza's too.

## THE RETURN HOME

SANCHO PANZA: Hold up your head, your worship. Cheer up, if you can. Thank heavens you didn't break a rib with that fall. Let's go home, your worship, and give over going about in search of adventures in strange lands. In fact, though your worship took the beating, am I not the greater loser, since I lost and island?

DON QUIXOTE: Here Troy was, here ill luck, not my cowardice, robbed me of all the glory I had won; here Fortune made me the victim of her caprices and the lustre of my achievements was dimmed; here, in a word, fell my happiness never to rise again.

SANCHO PANZA: I've heard it said that Fortune is a drunken cantankerous whore, and, worse, blind and therefore does not see what she does, nor knows who she casts up or down.

DON QUIXOTE: You're a great philosopher, Sancho, I don't know who taught you. But I can tell you nothing either good or bad comes about by chance, but by the special preordination of heaven. This is my destiny, Sancho.

SANCHO PANZA: Why not leave your arms hanging from the tree, sir?

DON QUIXOTE: Good idea, Sancho, let it be hung up as a trophy, and under it we will carve on the trees what was inscribed on the trophy of Roland's armour –

'These let none move
Who dare not his valour with Roland prove.'

Sancho, I think we should become shepherds while I'm forced to live in retirement. I'll buy some sheep and everything we need. I'll be the shepherd Quixotino and you the shepherd Sanchino and we'll roam the woods and groves and meadows singing songs here, lamenting in elegies there, and drinking the crystal waters of the springs.

SANCHO PANZA: All I know is that as long as I'm asleep I neither hope nor fear. Good luck to him who invented sleep, the cloak that covers a man's thoughts, the food that removes hunger, the drink that drives away thirst, the fire that warms the cold, the cold that tempers the heat, and, in short, the universal coin with which everything is bought, the weight and balance that makes a shepherd the equal with a king and a fool with a wise man. Sleep, I've heard say, has only one fault, that it's like death; for between a sleeping man and a dead man there's little difference.

DON QUIXOTE: Never have I heard you speak so elegantly as now, Sancho. I begin to see the truth of the proverb you sometimes quote, 'Not with whom you are bred, but with whom you are fed.'

SANCHO PANZA: Ha, master, it's not me who's stringing the proverbs now, they pour from your worship's mouth like spring water down a mountainside.

# HOME

*Enter the HOUSEKEEPER, the NIECE, and TERESA PANZA, leading Sanchica.*

TERESA PANZA: Look at the state of you, husband of mine, more like lords of misrule than governors of islands!

SANCHO PANZA: Quiet Teresa. You are all hooks and no bacon. I've money which is all that matters.

NIECE: What's this, uncle? Just when we were thinking you'd come back home to lead a quiet respectable life, you're wanting to go off and become a shepherd.

HOUSEKEEPER: And how do you think you'll survive out in the fields? The heats of summer, and the chills of winter, and the howling of the wolves? Stay at home, look after your affairs, go to confession and be good to the poor.

DON QUIXOTE: Quiet niece, housekeeper, I know my duty. Now help me to bed, I don't feel well. And rest assured, whatever I might be, I shall provide for you both.

NIECE: What are you saying?

DON QUIXOTE: I feel, niece, as though I'm dying. Call my good friends, the priest, the barber Master Nicolas, I need to confess and make my will.

*Enter the PRIEST and the BARBER.*

Good news for you, my friends; I am no longer Don Quixote de La Mancha, but Alonso Quixano, whose deeds once won for him the name of good. Now I am the enemy of Amadis of Gaul and the whole regiment of his descendants. I now hate the stupid and profane stories of knight-errantry. Now I see my foolishness, now, by God's mercy I'm in my right senses and I loathe them.

SANCHO PANZA: What, Don Quixote, sir, why are you saying this?

DON QUIXOTE: Because I am rapidly drawing near death, Sancho. Enough with jokes and play-acting, let me have a confessor. Man must not trifle with his soul in extremis. And while my friend the Priest is confessing me, let someone, I beg, go for the notary to make my will.

PRIEST: Alonso Quixano the Good is indeed dying, and now in his right mind. We may go in to him while he makes his will.

*Enter Notary.*

DON QUIXOTE: Item, it is my will that, regarding certain monies in the hands of Sancho Panza, whom in my madness I made my squire, let no claim be made against him; but if anything remains over and above, after he has paid himself what I owe him, the balance shall be his too, and much good may it do him. And if, when I was mad, I promised him the government of an island, so, now that I am in my senses, I would give him that of a kingdom. He deserves it, for the simplicity of his character and the fidelity of his conduct.

(*Turning to SANCHO PANZA.*) Forgive me, my friend, that I made you to seem as mad as myself, pulling you into the same error I fell into myself, that there were and still are knights-errant in the world.

SANCHO PANZA: Don't die, the most foolish thing a man can do is to die without good reason, without anybody killing him, or any hands but those of sadness making an end of him. Come on, get up from your bed and let's go to the fields as shepherds like we agreed. Perhaps behind some bush we'll find the lady Dulcinea disenchanted as happy as the day is long and as beautiful as a flower. If you're dying of sadness at having been defeated, blame it on me. Besides, you must have seen in your books of chivalry that it's quite common for knights who are beaten one day to be the victor the next. Come on, Don Quixote, sir, don't die.

CIDE HAMETE BENENGELI: Don Quixote signed the will, received the last rites, and died.

# WY PLAY HOUSE

## WEST YORKSHIRE PLAYHOUSE

The idea of **Don Quixote** was born out of conversations between Playhouse Artistic Director Ian Brown and Josep Galindo and Pablo Ley following the production of **Homage to Catalonia**, directed by Josep, at the Playhouse in 2003. This was to be an ambitious project and to enable the transfer of Cervantes' epic novel onto the British stage the Playhouse commissioned Pablo to work with renowned Irish playwright, Colin Teevan. Over the next two years Colin, Pablo and Josep carved out a play from the 900 page book, with support from designers, actors and the staff of West Yorkshire Playhouse. This exciting new adaptation is the result and we are delighted to be staging the World Premiere.

Since opening in 1990, West Yorkshire Playhouse has established a reputation both nationally and internationally as one of Britain's most exciting and active producing theatres, winning awards for everything from its productions to its customer service. The Playhouse provides both a thriving focal point for the communities of West Yorkshire and theatre of the highest standard for audiences throughout the region and beyond.

West Yorkshire Playhouse works regularly with other major regional producing theatres and companies including: **The Bacchae** (2004) with Kneehigh Theatre; **The Wizard of Oz** (2005), **Alice in Wonderland**, **To Kill A Mockingbird** (2006) and the forthcoming productions of **The Lion, the Witch and the Wardrobe** and **Peter Pan** with Birmingham Repertory Theatre Company; **Hedda Gabler** (2006) with Liverpool Everyman and Playhouse; **Wars of the Roses** (2006) with Northern Broadsides; **Flat Stanley** (2006) with Polka and **Ramayana** (2007) with Lyric Hammersmith and Bristol Old Vic.

West End transfers have included: **Ying Tong** (2004) to the New Ambassadors; **The Postman Always Rings Twice** (2005) to the Playhouse Theatre; the Olivier award winning **The 39 Steps** (2005) which is currently playing at the Criterion Theatre in the West End; **The Hound of the Baskervilles** (2007) at the Duchess Theatre and **Bad Girls – The Musical** (2007) at the Garrick Theatre.

www.wyp.org.uk